THE TEN
COMMANDMENTS
of RELATIONSHIPS

Other books by Catherine Cardinal, Ph.D.

The Ten Commandments of Self-Esteem

The Ten Commandments of Relationships

Catherine Cardinal, Ph.D.

Andrews McMeel Publishing

Kansas City

This book is dedicated to my clients,
who consistently reflect to me the hope and tenacity
of the human spirit.

The Ten Commandments of Relationships

copyright © 2000 by Catherine Cardinal, Ph.D. All rights reserved.
Printed in the United States of America. No part of this book may
be used or reproduced in any manner whatsoever without written
permission except in the case of reprints in the context of reviews.
For information, write Andrews McMeel Publishing,
an Andrews McMeel Universal company, 4520 Main Street,
Kansas City, Missouri 64111.

00 01 02 03 04 QUF 10 9 8 7 6 5 4 3 2 1

Library of Congress Cataloging-in-Publication Data
Cardinal, Catherine, 1953–
    The ten commandments of relationships / Catherine Cardinal.
        p. cm.
    ISBN 0-7407-0993-3 (hardcover)
        1. Interpersonal relations. 2. Interpersonal communication. I. Title.

HM1106 .C37 2000
158.2—dc21   00-035533

Book design by Holly Camerlinck

--- **Attention: Schools and Businesses** ---

Andrews McMeel books are available at quantity discounts with
bulk purchase for educational, business, or sales promotional use.
For information, please write to: Special Sales Department,
Andrews McMeel Publishing, 4520 Main Street,
Kansas City, Missouri 64111.

CONTENTS

THE TEN COMMANDMENTS OF RELATIONSHIPS

I.
THOU SHALT BUILD THY RELATIONSHIP UPON SOLID GROUND.

II.
THOU SHALT TOLERATE THY PARTNER'S SHORTCOMINGS.

III.
DEFINE CLEARLY THINE INDIVIDUAL ROLES.

IV.
CAST NOT THINE EYES UPON THE PAST.

V.
THOU SHALT BE A GENEROUS LISTENER.

VI.
RAGE NOT, LOSE NOT.

VII.
COVET NOT THE GREEN, GREEN GRASS NEXT DOOR.

VIII.
THOU SHALT AGREE TO DISAGREE.

IX.
LET THY PASSION GUIDE THEE.

X.
THOU SHALT ACCEPT LIFE AS IT IS.

ACKNOWLEDGMENTS

To Daniel Bushnell . . . thanks once again for your magnificent editing, your literary flair (particularly with the "Relationship Commitment"), and helping my inner writer to find her own voice.

To my agent, Frank Weimann, for his professional insight and continued support.

To my editor, Chris Schillig, for her expertise, support, and insightful advice.

To JuJu Johnson, Jean Zevnik, Maureen O'Toole, and all the folks at Andrews McMeel who are consistently warm, patient, and supportive.

Special thank-yous to the following for their support and contributions: Leslie Bricusse; the Cohen Family; Dr. Joani Essenmacher; Kathleen Madigan; Dr. Bobbi Liberton; Patrice Karst; Renee Yasny; the Ponikvar Family; Patrice Messina; Frank Dana, C. H.; Dr. Morris Netherton; Dr. Eric Best; Abigail Lewis and the *Whole Life Times;* Bill Thill; and my family in Cleveland.

And my warmest thanks to my extended family in Los Angeles (you know who you are). I love each and every one of you. Without your love and support none of this would be possible.

INTRODUCTION

There are deep undulating patterns that breathe through all of creation. Nature's laws reveal themselves in every leaf that falls and every bee that hums. Every living form is birthed on the scene, showers its glory for all to see, then wanes into seeming oblivion—only to reappear in another guise, for another time. Yet underneath this vast panorama of creation lies the sure, steady heartbeat of Life itself. Like a precise timepiece, its laws unfold with exactness and certainty.

Though it may not appear obvious, these same laws hold true in human interactions. Whether in business, play, work, or family, our relationships reflect the steady beat of natural law.

In earlier times humanity seemed more in tune with

the cycles of creation. There was respect for nature's seasons, time given for family rhythms, and fewer challenges to the dynamics of intimate relationship. As time moved forward and technology developed, our delicate balance tilted. Our progress, while providing us with greater comforts, has stripped us of certain basic instincts—instincts that clearly affect our personal and social lives.

While we can communicate around the world in a matter of seconds, we are less able to communicate with people in our immediate environment. Our divorce rate hovers at about 60 percent and it is common to be married two or three times in a lifetime.

What have we lost? With all the self-help books and TV talk shows, why can't we as a country make relationships last? What basic fundamental skills have gone by the wayside?

In my practice I see hundreds of couples struggling for answers. Often it's simply a matter of not knowing what to do or how to behave. There are many complex books and programs available, and they can be helpful. But I wrote this book of "Ten Commandments" to be a short yet comprehensive guide to creating a successful relationship. It highlights fundamental principles, and so is a quick, to-the-point, yet complete reference guide for the time-challenged.

Since most of our lives today are so hectic and demanding on our time and our psyches, we are not inclined to be fully present with our partners. We often feel overwhelmed and overtaxed, and it becomes all too easy to take our relationships for granted.

As tensions mount, it sometimes seems easier to throw in the towel and move on. But we carry our issues with us to the next person . . . and the next. At what point do we stop and learn how to create stronger relationships? I assume from the fact you're now reading this that you've arrived at that point. Congratulations! I believe there are certain basic rules that will bring harmony and balance into what seems to be a natural phenomenon, partnering with someone and working it out!

This book discusses ten techniques that I have found to be the most profound and yet practical means of creating successful partnerships. Modeled on the original Ten Commandments, these principles offer insight and wisdom for enriching our lives through more skillful relationships. When couples follow these simple guidelines, they experience greater happiness, longevity, and sanity in their primary relationship. May you find the same.

Commandment I

THOU SHALT
BUILD THY
RELATIONSHIP
UPON
SOLID GROUND.

Do you and your partner feel safe with each other? Do you believe your mutual bond is anchored in deep and abiding trust? Do you believe your relationship could survive any unexpected traumas?

A relationship is a living, growing, evolving thing. Considering that change is its most constant characteristic, learning to create stability in it becomes a priority. The way to ensure that a relationship survives long-term is to build it on a strong foundation.

How do you stabilize your foundation? There are no guarantees here, but there are some proven indicators of success. In my experience, four primary pillars support a successful long-term partnership:

1. Communication
2. Commitment
3. Shared Vision
4. Trust

Where is "love" in this list, you may ask? Well, actually love is woven throughout these four pillars. You cannot truly master any of them without love—love is the substance out of which they are built.

Communication

Couples must learn to communicate effectively if their relationships are to survive. Many partners find it easy to talk with each other at the beginning. This may be one of the reasons they were initially attracted to each other. But finding it comfortable to talk is no barometer for the depth of communication.

As any relationship matures, differences begin to emerge. If a couple's communication skills are limited, it's easy to get defensive, argue, and fight. And, if not checked in time, such a breakdown can lead to separation.

One technique that I've found especially helpful in

these cases is what I call proactive dialogue. With proactive dialogue, both partners assume responsibility for (a) expressing their real feelings, needs, and wants; and (b) at the same time not alienating or hurting their partner's feelings and self-esteem.

When speaking, each person assumes an attitude of harmlessness and uses a positive tone of voice. He or she is careful to choose words that are not defensive, combative, or hurtful. For example, instead of an angry "You don't ever listen to me and I'm sick of it," you might calmly say, "It would be helpful for both of us if we could learn to be more open and communicate without yelling. Could we at least try to sit down and listen to each other?"

I recommend that a couple sit in chairs across from each other and practice proactive dialogue for fifteen minutes at least once a week. Each partner takes a turn speaking, expressing her or his real feelings but always carefully framing the words in a nonjudgmental way. This is not just a free-flowing outpouring of feelings but rather a consciously chosen method of emotional expression. The one listening agrees to welcome the information, digest it, and then actively collaborate on an effective solution to the problem.

At first doing this may seem like learning a new language, but the results are well worth the effort. Remember, your partner is your ally, not your enemy. (If you currently see your partner as an adversary, then it's time to do couple's therapy or reevaluate your relationship.) Communication is one of the most prevalent problems among couples today. Learning to build bridges through safe and skillful dialogue is imperative to maintaining a loving and lasting relationship.

Commitment

When two people reach the point where they are ready to commit to each other, it is important that each partner understands what the other's idea of "commitment" is. Their definitions must be congruent and their ideologies compatible; otherwise it will be difficult to establish a firm foundation for a lasting relationship.

Some people feel that true commitment cannot take place without marriage. Others believe that living together is as strong and meaningful a bond as marriage vows. This is a matter of personal choice; there are no rights or wrongs here. What is important is that both parties share the same viewpoint.

Among my clients is an unmarried couple who have been living together for fifteen years. They have an eleven-year-old child and are totally committed to each other and their relationship. But other couples I see have remarked that during tough times, they would have abandoned ship had it not been for their marriage vows. Commitment is an agreement between two people and is unique to each couple.

Shared Vision

Shared vision requires that both partners have reasonably similar ideals, values, ethics, goals, and life direction. This "compatibility factor" must be present for long-term growth potential. If the gap on any of these major issues is too wide (especially in the area of integrity), there will eventually be hurt, anger, and possible separation.

It may take a while to know if you and your partner share the same vision, but it is worth finding this out before making a long-term commitment. It is sad to see couples come together with great hope and expectations, only to realize that they are actually headed in different directions. This is especially traumatic when children are involved.

So take time to discover your real inner values and goals in life. Ask your partner to do the same. Reading books on self-discovery and self-improvement, taking classes, and finding a skilled counselor can help you both come to a clear understanding of yourselves. This inner search will give you a much more solid basis for entering a serious relationship.

Trust

When there is trust between two people, miracles can happen. I believe there is no greater experience, no finer feeling than being able to be fully yourself without being judged, critiqued, or mistrusted. When your partner is on the same page as you, trusting you with the same intensity, then love flourishes.

And when trust has been broken, the magic stops. We contract and become fearful, mistrusting, and doubtful. We all know instinctively when there is trust and when there is not. But what are the elements that build trust? Here are some of the attitudes and behaviors I've seen operating in successful relationships in my practice. These are simple steps you can take to build or rebuild trust in your partnership:

Keep your word . . . walk your talk

Tell the truth . . . always

Be open . . . and willing to be vulnerable

Share your heart . . . and listen to the other's

Criticize constructively

Temper your temper

Surrender graciously

Understand . . . and be kind

The moral of this story is: Trust and be trustworthy. The safety you create together will determine the quality of life you share.

From my clinical experience, it appears that all four of these pillars must be present for a relationship to remain healthy and endure.

Marlene and Lance, ages twenty-five and twenty-six, came to me, hoping to save their very damaged marriage. They were arguing daily, and both were exhausted.

They had met three years earlier and had gotten engaged after only seven weeks of dating. Six months later, they married. But after ten months their many differences began to surface. Because of their youth and lack of life experience, they didn't have clear pictures of themselves, let alone of each other. At this point, they were like strangers sitting across from each other in my room.

Within a few sessions it became obvious that their values, desires, styles of communication, and levels of maturity were vastly different. Each was a "work in progress," maturing nicely, but the two were growing at different rates and in different directions. They realized the thoughtlessness of their premature choice to marry and chose to separate.

Marlene went back to school, and Lance accepted a job in another city, but they remained friends. They had learned the valuable lessons that foundations take time to build and that emotions, youthful eagerness, hormones, and whimsical discussions are not the materials on which a mature, long-term relationship is built.

A strong foundation can be built at any point during a relationship. Some couples put in their four pillars only after years of frustration and trauma. However, for Marlene and Lance, the missing pillar was shared vision—and since they had jumped into marriage without doing their homework, their innate differences precluded making a successful marriage together.

These pillars will guide you in wisely choosing your future partner—or in enhancing the relationship with your present one. Creating a successful partnership is not easy, so take your time, build carefully, and treat this as a lifetime investment. The dividends are huge!

My cousins Carol Ann and Bill have been married for thirty-two years. They have two children, Beth and Bill Jr., both in their late twenties. Beth is happily married, has a great job, and has just had her first baby. Bill Jr. is successful and happy in his work. Carol Ann and Bill's children are both mature, balanced, and happy individuals.

I asked Carol Ann what her secret is. She responded, "Marriage is never stagnant. It is a dynamic cocreation. It's like a seesaw and requires constant give and take. There are times when one of us is weak in one area and things are thrown off balance. It's then that the other compensates until we feel we've found our balance again, our stability."

"Bill and I complement each other and know that if we went our separate ways we wouldn't find anything out there that we don't already have. We are comfortable with each other, honest and open in our feelings, and we have a deep, loving bond. We plan on spending our next thirty-two years together."

So all you skeptics out there, see what a firm foundation can create in your relationship. When built pillar by pillar, a relationship can become your home—a place of lasting nourishment, safety, and fulfillment.

Resolutions

1. Use the four pillars as a checklist when evaluating your relationship. Discuss them openly with your partner—and agree to take any corrective steps necessary to enhance the quality of your relationship.

2. Note any specific areas of weakness—and, just as you would take a specific supplement to correct a health imbalance, try to find the appropriate books that will nourish this weak aspect. Also, you might check out tapes, seminars on the subject, or a skilled counselor.

3. Put into practice the proactive dialogue technique described in this chapter. Agree to use it on a regular

basis, and, if necessary, seek a counselor or trusted friend to act as a neutral adviser.

4. Do your homework to build, and then give yourselves permission to turn your relationship over to a Higher Power (whatever that means to each of you). It can feel like an overwhelming burden to think we have to do all this work ourselves. This process is used in numerous twelve-step programs and is very effective.

Love does not consist in gazing at each other,
but in looking outward together in the same direction.
ANTOINE DE SAINT-EXUPÉRY

Commandment II

THOU SHALT TOLERATE THY PARTNER'S SHORTCOMINGS.

Do you recall the first time you met your partner—how beautiful he was in your eyes, how gracious, how kind, how talented? And on your first date, did she not leave you speechless with her charm, her energy, her sheer radiance? And did you not think how "perfect" this person might be for you?

Then, as time went on, you began to perceive slight "human" traits in your partner—subtle blemishes on the "perfect" image you were holding in your mind. And as your relationship became more settled, each of you most likely discovered aspects of the other that at first were bothersome, then annoying, and finally intolerable. You discovered the meaning of the saying "Even cream of wheat has lumps!"

How does this happen? The answer to this question contains one of the keys to successful long-term relationships. It's called crossing the bridge from romance to love, or from romantic love to human love. It may be true that marriages are made in heaven, but they are lived out on Earth. And that means we must learn to love people with seeming imperfections.

It's doubtful that there is a flawless mate "out there" for anyone. And even if there were a flawless mate for you, you would not perceive him or her as such until you had cleared up your own imperfect vision. So most people find themselves in relationships that have some degree of frustration or disappointment.

I've found several techniques useful in helping couples deal with this issue. First of all, we must keep in mind that what is a flaw for one person may be an asset to another. The habit of smoking may be intolerable for one person—yet for a smoker it may be a very desirable trait in a partner. How, then, does a person decide just where to draw the line?

I suggest that everyone learn to distinguish between flaws and fatal flaws. *Flaws* are those behaviors and habits that we learn to accept and tolerate in our partners. *Fatal flaws* are those traits that are simply unacceptable to us in a primary relationship.

So we begin with the understanding that every relationship will have its flaws—the question is simply, "Are they flaws I can live with or not?" It is helpful for you to know up-front what qualities are on your "fatal" list. Having this knowledge will empower you in knowing who you are and where your boundaries lie, and it will save you much time in finding and creating a lasting relationship.

Janeen, a very successful client of mine, had been involved with Martin for about three years. She traveled extensively, but they would manage to spend at least one to two weekends a month together, and occasionally he'd fly to meet her in various cities. His schedule was more flexible than hers, so he made a sincere effort to be there for her.

Janeen often referred to Martin as her "best friend." While on the road, she felt safe in calling him with any problem regarding her job. He always had good advice and was a generous listener.

Janeen knew that there were issues with Martin that required some attention. He still lived at home, and although he worked full-time for his parents' company, they paid him little. She wondered how they could ever raise a family on his salary. But she felt these issues could be worked out.

As time went on, however, Janeen began catching Martin in little white lies. At first, some money was missing. Then his whereabouts on a particular weekend and his friendship with a woman they both had known for years came into question.

Martin was a "good talker." He came in for a couple's session once, and I saw how smooth he could be. Janeen became increasingly confused, and I supported her in getting to the bottom of it all before she considered marrying him. Finally, through a girlfriend of hers, the truth came out. Martin had been leading a double life. He was carrying on a relationship with Janeen, speaking of love, marriage, and children, while seeing Tina and promising her the same "happily ever after."

Janeen, heartbroken, ended the relationship immediately. She had been willing to work through the financial issues—and was even open to tolerating the few white lies. But she knew Martin's duplicity was a fatal flaw for her.

We cannot always know everything up front. Many times a relationship surprises us as it evolves, with discoveries about our partners that were not apparent at the outset. A healthy relationship is not static but is a living,

evolving energy that brings us new awareness and skills as we participate in it.

Conflicts will emerge over time—and how we deal with them will be a measure of our success in relationships. One very useful trait in this regard is to discern your partner's willingness to engage in this process. Does your partner acknowledge that his or her behavior may be an annoyance to you? Is he or she willing to work with you on resolving any friction? If your partner is unwilling even to listen to what upsets you, that may end up on your fatal list.

Two friends of mine are young professionals. They lead busy lives and especially value the time they have together. Each is careful not to criticize the other—but they found that each had habits that began to grate on their nerves. She cracked her knuckles; he cleared his throat and blew his nose often. After quietly tolerating these habits for a time, both decided to talk about them. Neither one chose to stop

the behaviors, but they found a workable solution. If they wanted to indulge their habits, they would leave the room first. If that was not possible, they would first say, "Excuse me," thus acknowledging their partner's needs. Each partner now felt respected and, in time, learned to tolerate the other's behavior.

If you find that your mate is willing to listen and begins to take steps toward resolution—however small!—be grateful and supportive. If you find him putting the toilet seat down or see her not touching up her makeup while driving on the freeway, this means you were heard and your partner cares about you and the relationship. So get off his or her back. No one likes to be criticized while making an effort to improve.

Most relationships will have some degree of friction, often in daily routines. If your partner is willing to take steps to reduce the "annoyance factor," then you have a

healthy partnership. If the friction becomes severe and you find yourself in a stalemate, then perhaps couple's therapy is in order. I have seen many couples save their marriages by being willing to learn some basic relationship skills.

No partner is without flaws. Yet when you are willing to talk about the lumps in your relationship and do your part to smooth out the cereal, you will discover deeper love, keener respect, and more personal growth than you may have imagined possible. And being willing to see your mate with deeper love, understanding, and respect, you just may find that you are looking at your "perfect" partner.

RESOLUTIONS

1. Take the time to contemplate what you want in a relationship. What would it look and feel like on a day-to-day basis?

2. Then make a list of your own positives. What are those qualities, benefits, skills, and gifts that you bring to a relationship? Why would a partner choose to be with you?

3. Now list those qualities you would class as fatal flaws. Be sure that you are not just wanting an ideal image or are unwilling to deal with personal growth or learning to be tolerant. Ask yourself with each one the following question: If I met a person who had every desirable trait I

wanted and yet had this one flaw, would I be willing to work it out?

4. Finally, make a list of your own negative traits—what others might consider flaws. Are there any that you feel should be worked on? Maybe the effort to improve yourself will attract the "perfect" partner to you more quickly!

The question is not what a man [woman] can scorn, disparage, or find fault with, but what he [she] can love, value, and appreciate.
JOHN RUSKIN

Commandment III

DEFINE CLEARLY
THINE INDIVIDUAL
ROLES.

Are you happy with the role you have chosen in your relationship? Are you seeking to be cherished and loved by your mate, or are you more interested in being respected and appreciated? Are you aware of the subtle nuances of male and female roles and how these energies blend in the dance we call intimacy?

In order for a relationship to be balanced and whole, one partner must express more "male" energy (i.e., logical, assertive, dominant, left brain) and the other more "female" energy (i.e., intuitive, passive, receptive, right brain). Typically, men have chosen the "male" energy and women the "female" energy. Thus, the man's primary need is to be "respected," and the woman's is to be "loved and protected."

It's fine, however, for couples to reverse these traditional roles. I know of men who prefer the "female" role, while their wives are happy with the "male" role. The important thing is that their choice of roles is made consciously and is mutually agreed upon. For without this delicate balance of energies, confusion often occurs. . . . You can end up with two males sparring for power or two females feeling hurt and unsafe.

Before the Sexual Revolution, male and female roles were more clearly defined by society. The man went out into the world and made money; the woman stayed at home and nested. There was little deviation from this structure. But since the sixties, these roles have begun to blur.

Women needed to "liberate" themselves from their traditional expected roles. They forged out into the workplace, often displacing men in search of validation and esteem. Men began to pursue their softer, more intuitive side, often taking on parenting and housekeeping chores. Women were sporting power suits as men began donning aprons.

Roles in relationships shifted accordingly. There were no longer the traditional rules. It became okay for the woman to be the aggressor and for the man to be passive. Each gender began to explore all the options. Although this new freedom felt liberating, it also created a fertile field for battle between the sexes.

Carol and Luke had a five-year relationship that was extremely rocky. It took only a few minutes of their first session for me to see the problem.

When they met, Luke's career was flourishing—success had come quickly to him. Carol's career was just starting and was not yet at the level of Luke's. The first two and a half years of the relationship were great. Their roles were well-defined, and they were both capable and comfortable in those roles: Carol being the female polarity and Luke the male. Luke paid for all their dates and trips together, and enjoyed his ability to provide for both of them. Carol was comfortable allowing him to lead, and she felt safe, loved, and cherished. She nurtured him and had a great deal of respect for him and his choices.

Then Luke's career started to wane and money became a problem. Carol gladly offered to pitch in and do most of the providing, because her career was now on the rise. She was content to switch roles, trusting that Luke's career would soon be back on track. But his career did not bounce back.

Relying on Carol made Luke somewhat uncomfortable, and he began to show signs of depression. He tried in vain to revive his career and shunned her suggestions of ways to pursue new jobs in his field. Carol felt that by offering advice she was assisting him in taking back his male role, but Luke felt "disrespected and put down."

Carol become increasingly frustrated with this reversal of roles. And Luke deeply resented the situation as well, seeing Carol's career success as a daily reminder of his own perceived failure. Not long into their counseling work, they ended the relationship—mainly at Luke's prompting. Not being able to resume his male role was simply too much for him to handle.

According to Carl Jung, every man has a feminine intuitive side and every woman has a masculine thinking side. So, it could be said, whenever a couple comes together there are four people involved—the male and female sides of the man, and the two sides of the woman. This, of course, would apply to gay couples as well.

During the course of a relationship, it is natural for each partner to express both—as long as one partner maintains the dominant role most of the time. If Luke's "downtime" had been shorter, Carol's taking on the male role temporarily might have worked out.

I have two friends, Jake and Laura, who have a great

relationship. He is the male and she, the female. But at times, such as when Jake is ill or having a rough time at work, Laura will say, "Don't worry, honey I'll take over now. You just rest and get better." She gives him the space to be receptive and go inward while she "keeps the wolf away from the door."

Later, when he feels better, Jake lets her know, "The man of the house is *back!*" At this point Laura usually dresses up in something extra-silky and revealing, and they have passionate sex. Laura told me that at these times she feels the most loved and honored . . . the most "womanly."

One afternoon she came to see me looking exceptionally radiant. "A little afternoon delight?" I ventured. "Honey," she replied, "if I could bottle and sell what that man does for me, we'd all be rich. He is *all* man!"

Equitable assignment of roles is necessary in every relationship. Some critics tell me that these are outdated techniques and don't apply to society today. Others claim they are antiliberation. But after sixteen years of practice, of hearing women complain that "I don't feel safe or cherished," and men complain that "she doesn't respect me and nags all the time," I *know* many couples are suffering from lack of clear role definition.

Here is one method you can use to help you clarify your roles. For the man, you must know that a woman above all wants to be sure that her nest is safe. *Nest* here can mean home, family, emotions, integrity, and so on. So you must listen to her and provide her with the elements that create safety. For example, if punctuality is important to your woman, you must make every effort to plan well and not be late. This is a form of thoughtfulness that will help her to feel safe.

Now for the woman, you must ask the man for what you want and not expect him to be a mind reader. As an example, a client of mine was angry that her boyfriend did not offer to help her around the house when he stayed over for the weekend. She felt he was taking her for granted. When I asked her if she had actually requested his help, her reply was, "No, but he should know . . . he should offer."

The first thing I asked her to consider doing was removing the word *should* from her vocabulary. *Should* is a negative word that often implies guilt and shame. I suggested she replace it with *could* or *would* and then repeat the sentence about her boyfriend. She thought for a moment and then offered, "I wish he could know that I would appreciate his help."

"Excellent!" I responded. "Now—just how 'could' he come to know this?"

"Well, I suppose I could ask . . ."

The following week she reported that her boyfriend had turned into "Mr. Handy Man." She did ask him for help—and he revealed that, because her house was so neat and tidy, he assumed she had everything handled so his job was to be with her and keep her company. Once he knew she wanted his help, he was thrilled to be of service and couldn't wait to help her out.

So, ladies . . . ask clearly for what you want. If your man refuses, he may well not be the right man for you. But if he responds and fulfills your wish, *praise him!* If he is taking the steps to make you feel safe (i.e., doing what you ask), then take the time to appreciate him (i.e., make him feel respected). This is what I call "the loop that works." If you find yourself in a loop that doesn't work, where one of you feels unloved and unsafe and the other disrespected and made to feel wrong, then take a look at your respective roles. Talk openly about your feelings and what is happening. Take the time to clear up role confusion—and watch the healing that follows.

Every one of us has a deep need to love and to be loved. Have you known anyone who did not yearn for romance, for love, for "happily ever after"? When we were children, fairy tales filled our minds and hearts with hopes of true and lasting love. As adults we find that relationships are difficult—but, from what I've seen, being alone is next to impossible.

So in today's world of complex dimensions, immediate gratification, and head-spinning velocity, relationships can be a source of peace, of stability, of foundation. Defining roles is a major key. Put it to work in your life—and you'll have a much easier time with relationships. It won't be long before your friends start asking you for advice.

Resolutions

1. Take some time for serious introspection. Examine all the areas of your life in relationship and decide in which areas you prefer to play the female role (receptive, cherished, right brain) and which the male (assertive, respected, left brain). Be very honest with yourself—and remember that who you are at work does not have to be who you are at home.

2. Consult with your partner and be clear on what role or roles he or she plays in the relationship. Indeed, there is a balance of aspects between you. If you find an imbalance, you may discuss with your partner the possibility of assuming different roles in certain areas. Remember

that a healthy relationship requires one partner to be pre-dominantly "male" and the other predominantly "female."

3. If you are the female polarity, you first need to be clear with yourself about what you want and need. Then brush up on your communication skills. How well do you communicate your needs to your partner? Are you feeling loved, cherished, and safe? Ask him or her for feedback and suggestions.

4. If you are the male energy, be sure that you are feel-ing respected and appreciated. If not, perhaps she is not communicating well with you. Examine yourself—are you clear about her needs, and are you willing to fulfill them? If not, you'll need to find out why. Are you doing everything you feel necessary yet finding that your part-ner's needs seem insatiable? Whatever issues arise, be

sure to keep all lines of communication open to discovering "the loop that works."

5. Be flexible and willing to switch roles when the situation calls for it. The give and take of male/female energy is a vital part of a healthy and sane relationship.

*Good family life is never an accident but always
an achievement by those who share it.*
JAMES H. S. BOSSARD

Commandment IV

CAST NOT THINE EYES UPON THE PAST.

Do you have a sense that your current relationship is haunted by your past? That there are certain "ghosts," in the form of childhood memories, previous partners, past wounds or traumatic events, influencing your present-day life? Do you find yourself experiencing lingering resentments?

Each of us has a tendency to hold on to the past. People and events that hurt us or caused us to feel alone, betrayed, or frightened stay lodged in our conscious and unconscious minds. In each of us lives an inner child who feels all of these complex feelings. Sometimes it becomes difficult to distinguish what is past from what is present reality.

These past patterns continue to subtly influence our behaviors and choices, especially in the area of relationships. Perhaps you find yourself reacting to your partner in ways that are carryovers from past partnerships, or even earlier, from childhood conditioning.

Your unconscious mind does not discriminate in time and space. It simply responds to stimuli. If a current situation resembles a scene from your past, your mind will revert back to that scene. You will find yourself responding in similar ways to your earlier memories.

Our minds tend to free-float from time to time with little or no conscious effort. One moment we may be acting our current age, and the next we may regress to being a fifteen-year-old. If you look closely, you will begin to discern inconsistent patterns of behavior in both yourself and your partner.

For most of my life, I had an irrational fear of men in uniform, especially tall men. If I was casually walking down the street and saw a policeman, I would instantly feel a weakness in my knees and suddenly be afraid. I always assumed this was simply a result of watching too much violence on TV as a kid.

During a therapy session that involved regression to

my childhood, I returned to my first day at kindergarten. I recall being very frightened and not wanting my mother to leave me there. She walked me to my seat, sat me down, then proceeded to the back of the room. I began crying uncontrollably.

Suddenly, a huge hand appeared before my face and slammed down on the desk. A sharp voice screamed, "Be quiet!" I looked up in terror, and before me loomed a very tall priest (over six feet), wearing a long black robe. He looked like a cross between the devil and the Jolly Green Giant. His hands were each the size of my head.

The shock of his hand slamming down in front of me, his booming voice, his towering physique and black robe shut me up at once. I was terrified. My mother was asked to leave the room. And I began that adventure known as kindergarten.

I never consciously understood where my fear had

come from before. But by recalling this incident in therapy, I experienced a release from its emotional imprint. I realized that whenever that fear was activated, I was responding as my five-year-old self. After my therapy session, I never again felt fear around tall or uniformed men.

This inability to stay completely present can result in misreading any situation and then responding inappropriately. I recommend if you find yourself having irrational responses to situations that you check in with a competent therapist and seek the source event. You'll be amazed at how such a simple process can profoundly change your ability to make present choices.

As an alternative you might discuss your past with your partner (or a close friend or family member) so that any old patterns you are carrying will be revealed and you can let them go. Until you consciously let go of old grievances with mother, father, siblings, or friends, you will

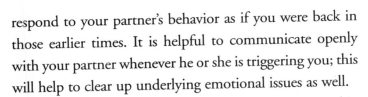

respond to your partner's behavior as if you were back in those earlier times. It is helpful to communicate openly with your partner whenever he or she is triggering you; this will help to clear up underlying emotional issues as well.

Other ghosts that may haunt your current relationship are hurtful things your current partner may have done to you. For instance, if your mate committed some indiscretion in the past but has realized the error, is remorseful for the harm caused you, and is trying to make things right, then it is up to you to forgive and let go. The degree to which you're holding on to the past is the degree to which you're distorting your vision of the present (and the future). Let the past go! See your partner with fresh eyes each day.

There is a story of two monks who come to a river. A woman is standing on the bank, wanting help to get across. So one monk offers to carry her, since they are going in the same direction. After crossing the water, the monk sets the woman down, bows to her, and the two monks proceed on their way.

After some distance has passed, the other monk stops and says, "I can't believe you carried that woman across the river. You know we are strictly forbidden to touch a woman, under *any* circumstances. I can't believe you did that!"

The first monk calmly replies, "My dear brother, I put that woman down on the other bank of the river a while ago. It is you who are still carrying her."

The key here is to work diligently on honoring the present moment. Learn to let go of grievances from childhood, wounds from previous intimate relationships, and prior hurts from your current partner. Divorce yourself from past resentments. Give yourself the gift of a fresh and invigorating future. Live each new day with hope and optimism, and build together a life that one day will become sweet memories in your heart.

Resolutions

1. Take note of the times you have experienced an irrational response to a current situation. Ask yourself what age you might be in that moment, and trust the first age that comes to your mind.

2. If you can recall what happened at that age, journal about it and discuss it with someone you feel safe with—a friend, partner, or family member. If you cannot seem to uncover a source event for your behavior, you may wish to seek the help of a professional.

3. Allow time for you and your partner to talk about the inner child who lives within each of you. Recognizing

this child's point of view in any situation can allow for much healing.

4. If resentment surfaces about something your partner has done in the past, and you've adequately discussed your feelings and your partner has acknowledged the mistake, then practice channeling that negative feeling into some other form of expression. Release it through exercise, gardening, singing, reading, dancing, meditation, or other activity. Learn to turn your negative emotions into a positive expression of the same energy.

5. Leave your past partners in the past and never compare your current partner with them. Nothing hurts quite like being negatively compared with a former lover. Forgive and forget—and appreciate your life (and your partner) in the present.

Today is a reality, for it's here and it's now.
And the young may dream of tomorrow, and the old may
sigh at the past.
But today is the sweetness and sorrow and the
only thing that will last.
For today is the day we are living and this moment
is all that we know.
And the things that we do, and the things that we feel
and the things that are true, and the things that are real.
All our hopes and our fears, all our laughter and tears
They're today things, not tomorrow (or past).
There is only today, and it never goes away.

ANTHONY NEWLEY AND LESLIE BRICUSSE

Commandment V

THOU SHALT BE A GENEROUS LISTENER.

Do you sometimes feel that you are misunderstood? That your partner is not "getting" what you're trying to say? Do you question your ability to communicate? Are you ever accused of not listening, of not really hearing? Do you and your partner ever argue about these issues?

If so . . . join the crowd! This is the number-one complaint I hear in therapy. "She didn't listen to a word I said." "He is constantly interrupting me." "She simply doesn't understand who I am." These are couples' counseling "classics." They reflect a very common problem— that of learning to be a generous listener.

Each of us is a unique bundle of very complex strands. As I mentioned in my previous book, *The Ten Commandments of Self-Esteem,* "We are each a result of our history plus our decisions. These two together create a matrix of patterns and beliefs that govern our thinking and our behavior." And, thus, our ability to listen and communicate.

To become a generous and accurate listener can be difficult because of our "filters." Filters are the results of our history and become the screens through which we receive our information. Over the years we have become masters at using our filters; we use them often, mostly unconsciously.

The problem is that our filters alter the information as it comes through. Just as a white stage light becomes blue when a blue filtering gel is placed on it, words passing through an individual's filter can turn into something totally different. What is white is perceived as blue.

So if your partner casually says, "I think that the bigger pan will be better to cook the spaghetti in," and you were constantly told you were stupid as a child, you may hear "Use the bigger pan, you stupid idiot!"

Each person needs to be diligent in figuring out his or her filters in order to hear what is *really* being said.

Only when we listen without our filters can we determine if we are being treated appropriately. Hearing our partner truly requires generosity and compassion. We need to "listen between the lines" and know how and when to respond.

Recently one of my friends, Libby, told me that her partner, Gene, had made a decision to do whatever it took to understand her. He was committed to work through any challenges they might have in their relationship. She noticed that a major part of his decision involved active, caring, and compassionate listening.

One evening she was upset about something in the relationship and couldn't isolate what it was. Gene asked what was wrong, sensitive to the slightest nuance in her voice and words. She replied unconvincingly, "Nothing," only because she wasn't clear enough to discuss it. He continued to ask what she was feeling and thinking, inviting but not pushing. Because of his sincere interest and repeated invitation, she was eventually able to fully explain what was going on.

Each interaction we have with our partner has a particular mood, a unique flavor. Sometimes it is wise to nudge a little, and other times it is better to sit quietly and receive our partner's message in its entirety. Certainly we need to avoid interrupting and rushing to get a word in.

One great listening technique is the "Floor Is Yours" exercise. Whenever the need arises, give each other a set time (ten to fifteen minutes or more) in which to talk freely—to vent and to let loose—*without interruption!* This works well, for example, when one partner has had a bad day at work or is having trouble with the kids. It's very healing just to talk nonstop, in a stream of consciousness, without any filters or hesitation—or any comment by the

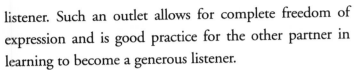

listener. Such an outlet allows for complete freedom of expression and is good practice for the other partner in learning to become a generous listener.

Listening requires a certain level of emotional maturity. Children constantly need to be the center of attention and will find many ways to let you know that! But as adults we strive to develop more effective communication and listening skills. We allow the people we love to take precedence, and we learn to be quiet, to hear, to understand.

One of my clients, Robin, told me a delightful story about her husband, Tom. They were working together on a project, and at one point she became weary and discouraged. "I was just bummed," she said. "He has more of that good old work ethic and can plow through no matter what mood he's in."

He asked, "What's wrong?" She told him that their work styles were just too different and she couldn't fit into his rhythm. She felt deflated and completely unmotivated. Yet the work still needed to be done.

He listened carefully to her, then made a suggestion. "Why don't we take a break, walk down to the beach, and bring the work with us?" Robin, who loves the ocean, was thrilled.

A few minutes later they were walking hand in hand, hearing the ocean roar and discussing the project. She later told me, "This wasn't a compromise that involved both people settling for less than they wanted. This was a totally satisfying solution that involved creative, active, and concerned listening."

As we move forward on this journey called Life, we hope we'll get smarter so that our road will become easier. Learning to listen is a major skill that not only lightens our load but allows us a deeper experience of Life. In partnership it eliminates preconceptions, which can lead

to painful misunderstandings. It allows us to build deep, genuine, and lasting relationships.

We all have a deep yearning to be heard, to be understood. With great reverence, learn to be still and listen completely to your partner. Learn to respond with wisdom, compassion, and understanding. Then feel that glorious elation that is reserved for those who have mastered the fine art of communication.

RESOLUTIONS

1. Pay attention to how often you interrupt your partner—and how often he or she interrupts you. Make a mutual commitment to break this pattern of behavior.

2. Practice the "Floor Is Yours" exercise on a regular basis. This will help both of you improve your communication skills.

3. If a discussion ever begins to escalate into an argument, make an agreement with your partner to take a "time-out." It's a good idea to agree on a time limit on the time-out—in the moment. Once each of you cools down, you may continue the discussion, calmly and in a spirit of compassionate listening.

4. Remember that your partner is not "the enemy." In most cases he or she simply needs understanding and some kindness. Your partner is asking to be heard, loved, or respected. Offer what he or she wants, and you may find the same love returned to you.

Few delights can equal the mere presence of one whom we trust utterly.
GEORGE MACDONALD

Commandment VI

RAGE NOT,
LOSE NOT.

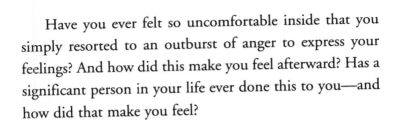

Have you ever felt so uncomfortable inside that you simply resorted to an outburst of anger to express your feelings? And how did this make you feel afterward? Has a significant person in your life ever done this to you—and how did that make you feel?

Is anger a primary feeling for you? Does it appear often in your relationship? It's natural for us to use anger as a means of expressing a multitude of feelings. Those feelings might include hurt, betrayal, frustration, disappointment, fear, humiliation, sadness, and loneliness. The list is virtually endless.

In the heat of an argument, it's often too difficult to know exactly what's going on inside of us, to identify what the other person did or said that triggered our reaction. Rather than confront the situation with understanding and self-control, we release our pent-up emotions through raging at our partners . . . which often encourages them to do likewise.

If not checked in time, raging can easily lead to words that are destructive. And words, once spoken, can never be erased. Without forgiveness they are difficult to mend. It's heartbreaking for me to watch a couple strive to heal the damage from cruel words spoken during a raging argument.

Raging is a lose-lose situation. The hurt and alienation that result from expressing rage are slow to heal. And slow healing is never healthy for a partnership. A relationship is delicate, much like a fine china cup. Occasional raging may crack the cup, and with time it may be mended. Ongoing rage breaks the cup. This is a "no heal" situation.

I received a frantic phone call from a man telling me his wife was on the verge of a nervous breakdown and asking if they could come in at once. I arranged for an appointment the following day.

When Lisa and Mark walked into my office, the tension was so thick between them that I could feel my stomach turn. They sat on opposite ends of the couch with jaws clenched and fists tight.

Mark told me, "I just can't get through to her and make her understand how I feel. It's driving me crazy!" At this point I realized that *he* was on the verge of breaking down.

I asked Lisa what was going on. She sank into the couch and replied, "Ask the police." It turned out that whenever Mark felt he was not being heard, he screamed and yelled in her face; then, when she tried to push him away, he resorted to physical abuse. The neighbors then called the police. This scenario was happening about once a month.

After hearing more details of the story, I asked them why they stayed together. Mark angrily responded, "I love her—why doesn't she hear me?"

I worked with Lisa and Mark for two years, both

separately and together. Mark's childhood was marred by an unavailable father and a domineering mother. Mom held the sole right to be angry. If Mark or his siblings expressed any anger, they were punished. So Mark was overflowing with unexpressed rage.

Lisa had been shuffled from foster home to foster home from age two until she was ten. She was then placed in an orphanage until she was eighteen. She had not an ounce of self-esteem.

Theirs was a difficult case, each partner needing careful monitoring. In the end, they split up. The words and physical abuse exchanged were too much to be healed. Their cup was shattered.

The paradox about rage is this: It's a healthy thing to express our anger! It feels good to blow off steam, to let it all out. Some people are actually addicted to the high that comes from a good outburst. In fact, in clinical set-

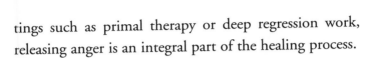

tings such as primal therapy or deep regression work, releasing anger is an integral part of the healing process.

However, raging needs to be kept in a therapeutic setting. There is no room for it in a relationship, for it unravels the delicate fibers that form the bond between partners. This bond is sacred—it must be honored and respected for any relationship to survive.

It is critical to determine if you or your partner has rage-aholic tendencies. A rage-aholic is someone with little or no control over angry or violent outbursts. Typically one partner's anger is always larger than the event that triggered it. So the other partner learns to walk on eggshells around the rage-aholic. And a wise friend, Phil, once taught me, "You cannot have a healthy relationship when you're walking on eggshells."

Sam and Bernadette came into therapy because of a breakdown in their communication. It started when

Bernadette opened some of Sam's mail. Her explanation was, "It looked like advertisements, and I didn't think you'd mind." He felt violated.

This set up a chain of events, which I call the "domino reaction." She began to worry constantly if she was violating his space. And he was vigilant and defensive about his privacy. Within a very short time they were tiptoeing around each other, nervous and anxious.

I worked with Sam and Bernadette on releasing hurtful feelings and setting new boundaries. Each had emotional maturity, and they were able to resolve their issues quickly. Their cup was only slightly cracked; within four sessions they were back on track.

If minor outbursts occur in your relationship, this is normal. Seek advice if you are unsure about appropriate severity. But if you are on the receiving end of rageaholic behavior, it's time for intensive counseling for both of you. If there is no commitment to change, here is a reminder from *The Ten Commandments of Self-Esteem:* "Thou shalt not consort with people who make thee feel bad about thyself." If you are unable to convert lose-lose behavior into a win-win, then you may need to seriously reevaluate your relationship.

Resolutions

1. To ensure a rage-free relationship, learn to stay connected to your true feelings. Take time out and go within to discover what your *real emotion* is. What are you *really* feeling—and why? Encourage your partner to do the same.

2. Find a time and setting for both of you to communicate the truth to each other—without any accusation, blame, or faultfinding. Create a space between you that is "safe" and allows for "truth telling." Focus more on how the other person made you feel—and possibly learn new ways of speaking or behaving that respects each other's "hot buttons." Over time this attention will lead

to more honesty, understanding, and communication with your partner.

3. If you find yourself with a rage-aholic, remember, first and foremost, that you are not causing the angry outbursts. A rage-aholic will always find some reason to rage. If it's not you, it will be the traffic, the children, the dog next door, whatever. Seek professional help immediately.

4. Set aside a portion of your day specifically for working out stress and pent-up emotions. We all have some degree of stress in our lives—and if not managed well it can develop into anger. Some suggestions for release are physical exercise, yoga, martial arts, meditation, crafts, or hobbies. Find a safe arena in which to release frustration and anger so you aren't bringing it into your home.

*Be not angry that you cannot make others
as you wish them to be, because you cannot make yourself
as you wish to be.*

THOMAS À KEMPIS

Commandment VII

COVET NOT THE GREEN, GREEN GRASS NEXT DOOR.

Do your senses reel at the sight of a perfect body? How about when you spot the flawless face, the one you've always been dreaming about? Does that set your desires on fire and your mind whirling with fantasies? And do you not unconsciously compare these qualities with your partner and find him or her lacking in some way?

Being envious of what others have, or appear to have, is a common problem. If our daily life seems like a series of rote tasks that we drudgingly carry out, then it's easy for ennui (boredom) to creep in. We may have the sense that everyone else is enjoying a life of utopian splendor while we are stuck in the mire of mediocrity.

From this state of mind, our perceptions are skewed. We see only a partial picture, and our minds exaggerate what's appealing. The tall man with the handsome eyes becomes Prince Charming next to a shorter, balding husband. And the woman who cooks like Martha Stewart is a goddess next to a domestically challenged wife. And on and on.

When we are desiring the great qualities of another, we are at the same time criticizing our partners—either verbally or nonverbally. As we move through our days noticing the most desirable traits in others, we end up creating an idealized composite of the most perfect human being imaginable. How could anybody ever hope to live up to that fantasy?

One of my clients, Greg, told me that he was involved with Annie for over two years. He said she loved him and he seemed to love her, but they fought often. He came in for counseling, complaining about "how sensitive" Annie was. "I try so hard to stop the fights, but we always end up arguing."

I asked him what he felt was going on, and he merely said that, because he was an artist, perhaps she felt threatened by his models, who were mostly beautiful women. We discussed other issues in his life, but after four sessions I asked him to bring Annie in with him.

Annie told me that whenever they were out in public, he'd comment on other women, saying, "Look at her legs—I'd love to paint her," or "Look at her breasts," or "Look at her perfect features." Annie added that Greg would often take note of the fine lines appearing around her eyes and mouth. Also, she had gained ten pounds, and he would make comments about her diet. Greg felt that he was not acting out of line, just being "artistically observant and supportive."

Annie said that their sex life was almost nonexistent and she was thinking of breaking off the relationship. She was only waiting to see if Greg made any progress in therapy. Greg eventually admitted that he was thinking often about other women's perfections and was increasingly disinterested in Annie. But because she was supporting him he unconsciously went into denial about his real feelings.

Greg did love Annie, but the way one loves one's mother. They split up, Annie off to find a man who loved *her* and Greg to find his perfect goddess. Annie remained in therapy; Greg did not.

Not wanting to settle for less is a healthy trait. But running through life unhappy with what you have chosen is disruptive and futile. And the truth of the matter is that behind every Prince Charming lies some other set of imperfections that your diminutive, hair-challenged husband doesn't have; your idealized domestic goddess may turn out to be shallow and unfeeling. You just never know!

My girlfriend had been married for fifteen years to the same man, her first and only lover. She, feeling she was missing out on something, became infatuated with her dance teacher. She thought of him often and fantasized about having a relationship with him.

One day after dance class, as she was leaving the dressing room, she overheard him on the office phone calling someone "a f—— bitch!" She peeked into the room and saw him punching the wall in a fit of rage. She ran home to her gentle, loving husband and made passionate love to him all night long!

In each of our lives imagination plays an important role. We use our powers of imagination to propel us forward to the next accomplishment, to envision and plan for our future, and to inspire us to grow and mature as conscious human beings. Without this inspiration, we'd quickly stagnate.

But in relationships imagination needs to play a different role. Its best use is in creating ways to better your communication, to visualize romantic evenings and vacations together, and to plan for a secure yet exciting future for your family.

Dwelling on images of perfection in other people is not healthy, constructive, or realistic. If your partner is wholly inadequate, then for both your sakes, move on. Otherwise, enjoy the fruits of your partnership—accepting that all partnering is flawed. One person cannot embody all ideal qualities.

So choose one partner and begin the process of commitment and growth. Doing it will challenge you yet bring you the deepest rewards. As the old saying goes, "He who is everywhere is nowhere." Learn to appreciate your own garden—water it daily with love and gratitude. And the flowers that grow and blossom will have a beauty that is rare, powerful, and uniquely yours.

RESOLUTIONS

1. Take stock of all the great qualities your partner has. Be honest and realistic. Share them with your partner if you like.

2. Notice whenever your mind wanders into fantasy. Ask yourself, "What is it in my life that feels so unfulfilled that I need to indulge in fantasy?" Perhaps you're bored with a particular task around the house, or maybe you've fallen into a routine with your partner and are looking for an escape. Remind yourself that there is no ideal mate or lifestyle that does not have its own set of challenges. Bring your mind back to your current reality—and begin the practice of enjoying whatever you're doing and whomever you're with.

3. Grant yourself permission to have a "little bit" of fantasy, but channel the energy you get from that fantasy into something constructive for you and your family.

We are haunted by an ideal life, and it is because we have within us the beginning and the possibility of it.

PHILLIPS BROOKS

Commandment VIII

THOU SHALT AGREE TO DISAGREE.

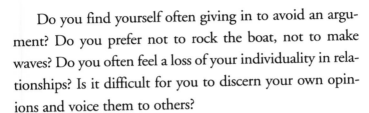

Do you find yourself often giving in to avoid an argument? Do you prefer not to rock the boat, not to make waves? Do you often feel a loss of your individuality in relationships? Is it difficult for you to discern your own opinions and voice them to others?

It is natural for us to disagree with each other from time to time. If you took any two people and placed them in a room together, it would not be long before differences would arise. This is the nature of human interaction. Our task is not to prevent this from occurring but rather to learn to master it in our daily lives.

Each of us carries a complex and unique history of experiences, and if we can open our minds and allow others' opinions and backgrounds into our awareness, we can enjoy richer, more fulfilling relationships. It becomes a delicate balance, maintaining our own sense of self while engaging with others and respecting their sense of self as well. Noah may have had the animals walking onto the ark two by two, but we can walk on our own and still be in partnership!

The person in a relationship who is the more nurturing is usually the one who works harder at not making waves. In an effort to keep the peace, she or he usually ends up sacrificing authenticity and being somewhat confused about who she or he is.

Molly and Brett came into therapy to discuss some issues affecting their marriage. Molly told me that she felt Brett was pulling back and not being as close with her, which made her feel insecure and unloved. Brett admitted feeling more distant and told me, "I still love her, but I feel like every day I lose a little more respect for her."

Molly flinched, shocked to realize this was what had been going on. She asked him, "Why?"

Brett replied, "When we first got together [two years earlier], I loved that you were always so willing to do what I wanted to do. If I asked you what restaurant we should eat at, you would reply, 'Wherever you want.' But now I feel that you just go along with everything. At a party, if we're discussing things with a group of people, you rarely say anything. But when I hear you talking on the phone with a girlfriend, you seem to have no problem talking about lots of things. Are you afraid of me?"

Molly started to cry, then turned to me and said, "You know, early on in the relationship I felt like I did express my wants and opinions, but they were always invalidated."

Brett was astonished at this and asked, "When?"

Molly continued, "Do you remember our first Christmas? We knew we weren't going to be with our parents. I suggested we drive up to Santa Barbara and spend the holiday there. You immediately said, 'Oh, no, Christmas is a holiday at home. Let's get a tree and spend it here, and invite some friends over.'

"The tone in your voice told me that this subject was not open for discussion. There were several other occasions when you did the same thing. So I learned it was just easier always to agree with you."

Molly then admitted that her father had made all the decisions in her house, and her mother had almost no input. For Molly to make any suggestions at all was a giant step forward, and when her ideas were not acknowledged, she fell right back into her mother's pattern of compliant behavior, not making any waves.

Brett had no recollection of the other occasions she spoke of and really hadn't known that she was taking the things he said so seriously. In his mind, all things were open for discussion, and he most likely could have been persuaded to go to Santa Barbara that Christmas if Molly had been more assertive and enthusiastic.

Molly and I worked on clearing up her mother's issues,

which lived inside of her, and she learned to be more expressive about what she wanted. Brett saw the changes in his wife and now felt that he had an "equal partner," in touch with who she is and what she wants. Now, eleven years later, they are still together.

When you don't express yourself and consistently honor only your partner's opinions, you lose yourself and may be causing your partner to have an inflated sense of self. This can well lead to problems; as in the case of Brett and Molly, a loss of respect can easily develop.

All of us have the right to express exactly what is in our hearts and minds, in a respectful way, and to allow our partner equal respect and the right to express themselves to us. When both partners share this understanding, there is a common bond of trust. Conflict and disagreement no longer are the wolf looming at the doorstep but remain an integral part of a healthy relationship. Differences, well-managed and embraced, become the catalyst for a mature and rich partnership.

So, both partners would do well to agree on a list of mutual commitments. Such a list might include the following:

Being unique and individual
Having strong, personal opinions
Honoring growth and evolution of the partnership
Staying flexible, open-minded, and open-hearted

It is not healthy to build a shrine to your own personal opinions, beliefs, likes, and dislikes. Neither is it sacrilegious to change your mind or to have your cherished beliefs challenged.

My friends Julia and Howard have been married for twenty years and have three beautiful, well-adjusted children.

When they met they found themselves at opposite poles politically. He lovingly referred to her as Big Red (she had a very liberal point of view), and she dubbed him Attila (he was more conservative).

Some of their first conversations were political debates, which would go on well into the night. Julia would enjoy baiting Howard's conservative friends, calling them Tory Englishmen. Howard was proud of her intelligence, strength, and ability to articulate her beliefs.

Julia felt the same way when Howard spoke to her more liberal friends. From the beginning of the relationship, they agreed that it was fun to be different and supported each other's need for expressing themselves. Over the years they have applied this principle to other areas of their lives, including disciplining the children, household duties, and balancing the budget.

When you agree to disagree, it must go beyond tolerating each other's opinions and reach into supporting each other's right to those opinions. You don't have to support or share your partner's beliefs; simply support his or her right to have and express those beliefs. And always keep in mind, just because you feel you're right does not mean that your partner is wrong!

Once you add mutual respect to your marriage, the fear of conflict disappears. What's left in your partnership, then, are two strong, self-reliant individuals who are prepared to be authentic and who have lots and lots to share with each other.

I can think of no more fitting words to conclude this chapter than those of Lucy (age twelve), the second of Julia and Howard's children. When asked what she did if she disagreed with one of her friends, she replied, "When I find that I differ from a friend, I will start up a conversation about it and find out why they feel the way they do. I want to know what they find interesting about it. It gives me pleasure to talk about it, and I always learn something new. Also, by not alienating that person, I usually end up with a closer friend."

RESOLUTIONS

1. Make an honest assessment of your need to be right. Whenever you feel yourself being self-righteous, undertake a self-examination. What is the tone of your voice? What are your feelings? And, most important, what is the primary emotion *underneath* your need to be right?

2. Ask your partner to do the same, and compare notes. See if you both have arrived at the same conclusions. Then set up "practice sessions," where you agree to discuss subjects on which your opinions differ, such as art, politics, religion, and sex. This works best if you both feel strongly about your opinions. Notice your behavior, your emotions, and your need to be validated as holding the right opinion.

3. Notice any tendency to hold back your opinions, defer to your partner, or keep silent at times in order to keep the peace. If you sense any such behaviors, discuss them with your mate. See if you can both work toward helping you express yourself more freely and assertively. If not, you may wish to attend classes or seminars or seek counseling in this area. Feeling free to express your authentic self is vital to the health and longevity of any relationship.

I have made a ceaseless effort not to ridicule, not to bewail, not to scorn human actions, but to understand them.
BARUCH SPINOZA

Commandment IX

LET THY PASSION
GUIDE THEE.

Are you passionate about your life? Do you open your eyes each morning and feel the juice of anticipation rushing through your veins? Can you hardly wait to dive into your day and begin doing what you love the most?

If not, perhaps this chapter is for you. Whenever people are in a state of passion about their lives, I call them "juicy." They simply bubble over with joy, and their effervescence is contagious. In fact, the word *enthusiasm* comes from the Greek *en theos,* meaning "in God" or "inspired." People love to be around someone who is on fire about life.

So how is it that we lose our juice? Usually it starts in childhood, where we're told what we can and cannot like by our parents and peers. If we really love music, for example, and our parents wanted us to go into medicine, they might unconsciously have tried to discourage us from pursuing our dream. From this experience we would have learned to suppress our true feelings and "settle" in later life.

When we enter into a relationship, a number of things can happen to further dampen our own juice. Most often, people begin a relationship with high hopes. There is excitement, promise, the expectation of a dream being fulfilled. However, as the initial thrill gives way to dealing with the day-to-day realities of getting along, then the "juice factor" begins to decline.

When we have to face problems about money, children, time, and in-laws on a daily basis, it's difficult to stay impassioned in relationship. It's then that tensions build, communication breaks down, and resentment sets in. At that point the excitement has gone—because there's not room for juice and resentment to exist at the same time. One will offset the other.

It's very human to feel disappointment at this stage—to feel stressed out, confused, contracted, even depressed. Arguments and stormy scenes occur too often. The dynamic between partners becomes tense and disharmonious. I always hope in these situations that the pressures that snuffed out individual passion will subside. Then both partners can rekindle their own inner sparks of joy and renew their special interests. And, like the phoenix rising from the ashes, their relationship can be reborn as well. Harmony and mutual respect can be restored—and life becomes juicy once again!

A good friend of mine, Maureen, had been married to one man for over twenty-five years. Their marriage, based on mutual love and respect, had survived well. Maureen adored William and seemed happy with their arrangement: he provided all the financial support, and she ran the home and cared for the children. He enjoyed his work and put in long hours. Often he would spend extra time with his friends playing golf or bridge. Although Maureen thought she was fine with their arrangement, she found herself daydreaming and beginning to read voraciously.

She confided to me, "I lived in a world of books, especially studying the history of art."

One night William was more than two hours late coming home—with no phone call. When he finally did arrive, having lost track of time with his friends, Maureen realized that there was a void inside her. Her self-esteem was low; she felt depressed often. She had her books to read but wanted more. William had so much passion for his life . . . what had happened to hers? Had the stresses of being a housewife and mother suffocated it?

"As I lay beside him in bed that night, I glanced at the photos of my children on the dresser. I took a pencil and began to sketch them. I was surprised and excited at my ability to capture their likenesses."

The next day she registered for a drawing class at the local college. William was very proud of her newfound passion and began to assume some of the household tasks, freeing her to attend art classes. Today Maureen is a truly accomplished artist.

"My passion for the arts has filled my life with enjoyment, creativity, and purpose. I took the reins of my life in my own hand, because I felt put down, and I found fulfillment. I did it for myself!"

Sometimes people try to use a relationship to cover up their inner lack of passion. A person who has not discovered and cultivated her or his own special brand of juice may unconsciously be drawn into relationship to try to avoid dealing with that issue. Such people may seek joy and fulfillment with another instead of with themselves. This usually leads to disappointment as well, for another person can never successfully fill gaps inside ourselves. Be careful as you enter into partnership that you are not falling into this trap. It's healthy to "clean up your own slate" before joining forces with another, because it's too easy for your own issues to become blurred by those of the relationship.

Some people's greatest joy *is* being in relationship with another. An intimate partnership is what they love doing the most. That's why it's best to know yourself well—a healthy relationship is always made up of two healthy individuals! Other people's special passions have been buried so long ago that they don't know what makes them happy. This usually implies a serious level of childhood abuse. For these individuals I recommend some type of therapy to help them go back and discover what makes them most fully alive. This knowledge is a birthright for all of us.

Whether in or out of a relationship, it is vitally important that you *not* let this happen to you. Nothing—no person, no problem, no stress, no circumstance is worth losing your passion over. *Nothing!* Keep your passion alive at all costs, and it will see you through even your darkest times.

Another scenario I see is one partner sacrificing his or her interest for the other. A common case is when one of them is an artist-producer or performer working on a project, or when one of them is just launching a new business. There is an excitement and frenetic energy about the project, and it's all too easy for the other partner to get caught up in that energy and lose his or her own focus.

About half of my practice is composed of people in the entertainment industry. In my work it's not uncommon to see men and women sacrifice personal passion to help a partner, to jump on the other's bandwagon and lose or neglect their own. This can be okay and even healthy on a short-term basis, especially if it's reciprocated later. But it can be a recipe for disaster as well.

Several years ago I was managing a full-time practice, finishing an advanced degree, and involved in a community chorus. My plate was full!

I became seriously involved with a man after dating him for several months. He, a writer and producer, decided to produce a stage show as a fund-raiser for the homeless. I agreed that it was a great idea and helped him hire a few people and solicit funds for the production.

What started out to be just a few hours of my time rapidly escalated into an almost full-time job. The people we hired were doing the best they could, but the show had grown quite large and required many hours of labor. I had an extensive background in theater, and, without noticing it, I began to assume many duties simply because I knew how to get the job done.

I ended up dropping out of school for a quarter, cutting back one day of work each week, and having less time to rehearse my numbers in the chorus. Not until the final week of rehearsals did I notice how tired and frustrated I had become. I had put *my* life and interests on hold to help with *his* project. Sure, it was for a great cause—but I had subtly sabotaged my own passion.

After the show was over, I reenrolled in school and got back on track. The show had cost me both emotionally and financially; I had to pay for an extra quarter of school. But the most important lesson I learned was just how deceptive another's passion can be, how that initial excitement can so easily draw you away from those activities that are really supportive of your own life direction.

So what's the answer here? How do we contribute to our partner's well-being and support his or her interests without giving up our own? The key to keeping our own juice alive while in a relationship is in setting and maintaining healthy boundaries. However, knowing this and applying it to our lives are two different things.

The problem is that we don't usually "jump" onto another's bandwagon—we usually creep onto it, inch by inch. The process is so subtle that we don't even notice it happening. Each day we become just a little more involved—until one day we wake up and find ourselves totally consumed!

Pay attention! Be alert to the subtle demands your partner places on you—and draw the line when necessary. Pay special attention to the unspoken demands on your time and energy, and act with awareness. Awareness provides the answers to most situations in life.

Finally, we do not have to be enmeshed in each other's lives. It's okay to have some separate interests. One of my dear friends loves musical theater, yet her husband does not. He loves sporting events—she does not. So she goes to the theater with me and other friends and takes a singing class at the local college. He goes to games and hangs out in sports bars with his friends. It works!

I believe there is a part of each one of us that is uniquely ours, and it is to be kept sacred within ourselves. I'm not

saying that we should keep secrets from our partners, but on a deep level each of us has a special inner resonance that needs to be respected, cared for, and developed. For that is our own recipe for inner passion.

Life is designed to be lived to the fullest. We are here on Earth to celebrate, not to contract; to express our gifts, not to smother them. By keeping our lives juicy, especially within relationships, we set a powerful example for others and contribute our own special note to the symphony of Life.

ℛESOLUTIONS:

1. Do whatever you must do to find your passion. Once you find it, take care to nurture it, honor it, and embrace it, and give yourself permission to express it fully.

2. Encourage and support your partner to do the same.

3. Be sure that your relationship and family needs are met in the process of tending your own personal passion.

True passion is the spirit of Life
wanting to express Itself uniquely as you.
DANIEL BUSHNELL

Commandment X

THOU SHALT ACCEPT LIFE AS IT IS.

Do you feel that life is worth living? As you add it all up at the end of the day, are you happy to be here? To be exactly who you are? Or do the struggles you endure as you carry your particular cross through life dampen your enthusiasm? Is it just too hard to "keep it all together"?

When you consider the following—

Crime

Disease

Pollution

Famine

Nuclear weapons

Biological warfare

Natural disasters

Financial problems

The suicide rate

Man's inhumanity to man—

it's a challenge to stay positive and cheerful! Sometimes it feels like we're on this major roller coaster, trying to hang on over seemingly impossible curves and treacherous drops, at times even dangling on the brink of death. Whew! How do we survive it all?

From my observation, there is one human trait that is most helpful in keeping us going. It's a thread that runs through most people's lives (though unfortunately not all). It's resiliency of the human spirit. This is our innate ability, from a soul level, to keep moving forward despite all odds, to continue striving toward excellence and growth despite countless obstacles.

For some, resiliency is easy to access. Whether blessed by nature or good parenting, these people tend to stay positive much of the time; they are always seeing the sunny side of things. Sometimes, this temperament is referred to as the sanguine type. Such people are always expecting success, and they rise like corks from beneath any waves of misfortune that may tend to depress them.

For others, resiliency is more difficult to access. These people are more predisposed to gloomy views, to seeing the negative side of situations, and they are usually anticipating the bad rather than the good. This temperament is often called the melancholic.

One sees the silver lining, the other the cloud. One perceives the rose, the other the thorn. One looks for the stinger of the bee, the other the honey. Certainly it's a blessing to be born with an optimistic personality. Such natures are invaluable and carry a breeze with them wherever they go. But for most of us, learning resiliency and a positive outlook takes some work. Still, the rewards far outweigh any effort involved.

As we master the skill of approaching life with a positive attitude, our chances for a more successful and healthy relationship increase. If you and your partner are both melancholic types, your relationship can work, but you may be simply doing the misery loves company dance. It's better for each partner to develop some capacity to digest life's unpalatable courses, find anchoring in hope, and cultivate inner joy.

If your partner feels down, you may help lift his or her spirits again—and vice versa. That is a much healthier dance. Most desirable is when both partners have learned that life can be tough and can still roll with the punches, not complaining but managing to have a good time. Theirs is a very rich relationship.

One of my friends came up with a great way to look at life on this planet. He calls it Club Earth. It's much like Club Med, where we plan a great vacation, looking forward to it with eager anticipation. We decide well in advance that we are going to have a great time. Whether it rains, our luggage is lost, or we find ourselves swimming in a school of jellyfish, we are *determined* to enjoy our vacation. After all, it's *our* vacation, *our* time to have fun, and *nothing* is going to stand in our way!

What a great attitude to have at Club Med! Why not join Club Earth? No matter what comes your way, make up your mind now that you will have some fun in the process. This applies especially to that intimate dance we call a relationship.

It's true that life here is polarized, a mixed bag of duality embracing our physical, emotional, mental, and spiritual selves. The pull of opposites is why this planet is so difficult to comprehend. Have you ever felt happy and sad at the same time? Or, if not simultaneously, in rapid succession? How about elated and disappointed? Excited and afraid? How can things here be so wonderful and so awful at the same time? The answer is . . . *POLARITY!*

It's everywhere! It's in everything and everyone. Most

religions of the world make some sort of reference to it. So let's get used to it, it's here to stay. Some friends and I were sitting around one night talking about what heaven must be like. After each of us shared insightful viewpoints, I added, "Heaven must be a place where there is *no* polarity!" Everyone agreed.

It's easy to feel anger and pain over the way life is here. I often hear the statement "It's so unfair!" And I agree—life in this dimension *is* unfair. I've spent my share of time working through the anger and pain I felt from my childhood, my relationships, and the deaths of people I loved. And for all of us, spending time in meditation, in church, or in therapy working through traumatic feelings is an important part of growing and maturing.

But there comes a point when we learn to accept life just as it is, the good and the bad. I often use this analogy with my clients. When you're shopping in a hardware store, it doesn't make sense to ask for a chocolate cake. You can yell and scream for one, but you will not get a cake. You're simply in the wrong store!

So when I hear people ask, "Why can't it all just be okay?" "Why do bad things happen?" "Why is life so unpredictable and seemingly unfair?" I remind them that throughout history Earth has been this way. Asking for it to be magically different is like asking for the chocolate cake in a hardware store. To lessen your frustration, accept the store you're in—figure out what you need there and move on. Use your time wisely.

Maybe one day Earth will be a utopia . . . all people loving one another, and the lion lying down with the lamb under clear, pollution-free skies in an environment of peace and harmony. But in the meantime we have to learn to be the best we can be while faced with the challenges we all face. Perhaps each of us has certain lessons to be learned here. Maybe there is a certain road each of us is destined to follow. God may be challenging us to learn and grow, to test our inner strength. These are questions that each of us must answer for ourselves.

One thing I know from my years of practice is this: making peace with what is, finding a way to work with it, being at a point of cause and not at effect, is the healthiest and most productive course of action I've seen.

When we are "at cause" in our lives, we are not victims. We are making clear, healthy choices from a place of good self-esteem. When we are "at effect," we are like a feather in the wind being blown aimlessly about with little or no choice. It's impossible, then, to have adequate control of our lives. But when we are "at cause," we stay on a more direct course and can handle life's unexpected twists and turns more gracefully.

One of my favorite stories is that of my friend Patrice's

eight-year-old son, Eli. Patrice is a single mom and faces many challenges raising Eli by herself.

One day while in the car together, Eli turned to her and, out of the blue, said, "Mom, it's okay to play the game, just don't let the game play you."

Astounded, Patrice calmly replied, "What do you mean by that?"

Eli answered, "It's like when you're playing a video game. You can really get into it, but you have to remember it's only a game."

Being "at cause" in your life often means being willing to seek emotional, psychological, and spiritual guidance. The couples who value each other enough to work on their personal issues typically have the healthiest partnerships. Clear yourself of your personal baggage and watch your life—and your relationships—flourish.

We are all white-knuckling it in some areas, hanging on

for dear life as our issues and circumstances toss us mercilessly around. Be compassionate for yourself, for your partner, for your children, for the entire human family. Allow yourself to see perfection within the imperfect, and order within chaos. Claim your share of humanity's tenacious, resilient Spirit, and support your partner to do the same. Together, through the eyes of love and acceptance, you will come to see the rightness and beauty that underlie all events, and find your rightful place in the grand scheme of things.

RESOLUTIONS

1. Take at least five minutes every day and find something to appreciate about your life. Some days this may be easy, and others it may be difficult. What matters is that you do this consistently. This is the gratitude exercise and it creates "an attitude of gratitude."

2. Encourage your partner to do the same. Share your thoughts and feelings.

3. Create a journal to record your thoughts and insights. Periodically review what you've written to observe how your feelings and attitudes change over time.

4. Start a program of inner discipline, such as meditation, prayer, or visualization, connecting you with your own Higher Power, to garner a deeper appreciation of life.

5. Spend time in nature with your partner on a regular basis. Let the natural beauty regenerate and rejuvenate both of you.

In every man's heart there is a secret nerve
that answers to the vibrations of Beauty.
CHRISTOPHER MORLEY

RELATIONSHIP COMMITMENT

And so . . .
I, _____ ,
Do promise to honor and cherish you,
My sweet reflection;
To respect and admire you,
My guide and companion;
To hold our togetherness sacred,
That through our bond we may grow,
Through our friction we may learn,
And through our friendship
We may fully celebrate Life
And give Love a home in our shared heart.